CW00394630

Three Shakespeare Songs

Ralph Vaughan Williams

Specially composed for
The British Federation of Music Festivals
National Competitive Festival
June 1951

MUSIC DEPARTMENT

OXFORD
UNIVERSITY PRESS

To Armstrong Gibbs

THREE SHAKESPEARE SONGS

for S. A. T. B. unaccompanied

R. VAUGHAN WILLIAMS

1. Full Fathom Five

The Tempest, Act I, Sc. 2

* *Note:* 'Ding', 'Dong' and 'Bell' should be sung

Di - ng
Do - ng
Be - ll

Copyright, 1951, by the Oxford University Press   Printed in Great Britain
OXFORD UNIVERSITY PRESS, MUSIC DEPARTMENT, GREAT CLARENDON STREET, OXFORD OX2 6DP
Photocopying this copyright material is ILLEGAL.

8

2. The Cloud-Capp'd Towers

The Tempest, Act IV, Sc.1

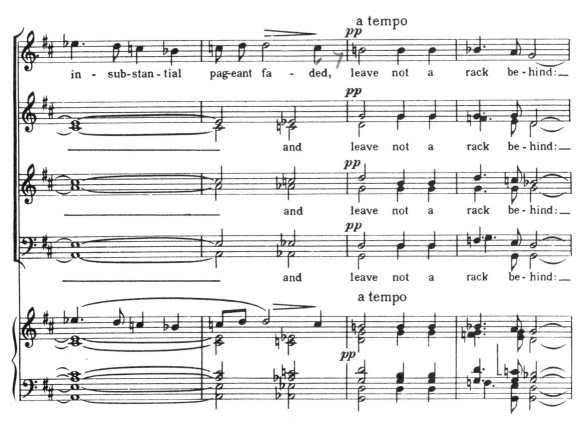

12

3. Over Hill, Over Dale

A Midsummer Night's Dream, Act II, Sc. I

light + nifty !

flood, tho-rough fire, I do wan-der ev-er-y - where, _____

flood, tho-rough fire, _____ O - ver hill, o - ver

flood, tho-rough fire, _____ O - ver hill, o - ver

flood, tho-rough fire, _____ O - ver hill, o - ver

Swift - er than the moon - è's

dale, Tho-rough bush, tho-rough brier, _____

dale, Tho-rough bush, tho-rough brier, _____

dale, Tho-rough bush, tho-rough brier, _____

seek some dew-drops here,___ And hang a pearl ___

dew ___ drops ___

dew ___ drops ___

dew ___ drops ___

in ___ ev - ery cow - slip's ear. ___

O - ver hill, ___ o - ver

O - ver hill, ___ o - ver

Tho-rough bush, tho-rough brier,
Tho-rough bush, tho-rough brier,
dale, O - ver
dale, O - ver
O - ver dale.
O - ver dale.
hill,
hill,

ISBN 0-19-343827-5

VAUGHAN WILLIAMS

Three Shakespeare Songs

Reproduced and printed by
Halstan & Co. Ltd., Amersham, Bucks., England